The Saning

the saning

LINDA ROGERS

Sono
Nis
Press

CANADIAN CATALOGUING IN PUBLICATION DATA
Rogers, Linda, 1944–
  The Saning

  Poems.
  ISBN 1-55039-099-6

  I. The Saning
PS8585.03953S3 1999
PR9i99.3.R65S3 1999

We acknowledge the support of the Canada Council for the Arts for our publishing program.
We acknowledge the assistance of the Province of British Columbia through the British Columbia Arts Council.

Cover and interior design by Jim Brennan
Edited by Barbara Colebrook Peace
Front cover photo of Sasha Rogers by Linda Rogers
Back cover photo of Linda Rogers with her grandchildren Sage and
  Sophie by Barbara Pedrick

Published by
SONO NIS PRESS
P.O. Box 5550, Stn. B
Victoria, BC V8R 6S4
sono.nis@islandnet.com
http://www.islandnet.com/sononis/

Printed and bound in Canada by
Morriss Printing Company Ltd.
Victoria, British Columbia

This book is for Dana and Brad, with love.

Thanks to my husband Rick van Krugel for his wisdom,
to Barbara Colebrook Peace for her editorial help,
to Jim Brennan for his sensitive reading of the poems and
rendering of the design, and to Dawn Loewen,
Heather Keenan, and Diane Morriss of Sono Nis Press.

Thanks also to the following who have given awards to poetry
in this collection: Mekler Deahl publishers (the Acorn
Rukeyser Award), The Canada Council, Arc Magazine, The
Cardiff International Poetry Society, Voices Israel, People's
Poetry, This Magazine and le Centre European Pour la
Promotion des Arts et des Lettres (Prix Anglais).

table
of contents

iii

the saning

children of paradise

Children of
Paradise

*The greatest evidence against the existence of God is
the suffering of little children.*

— **Fyodor Dostoevsky**

s h i   n
          e

This is how the child
  learns about gravity.
    First he is tossed in the air,
      his arms startling,
        beginning the swimming
          movement he knows by heart,
          music by a grieving
          composer he heard in the womb.

      O Welt ich muss dich lassen.

      Oh world I must leave thee,
    a poem by Brahms
  playing in his head,
 his fingers touching the ivory
teeth of martyrs
making their slow ascent
to the nacreous wall in heaven.

  The child orbits the earth.
  So long as the six million sing,
   so long as he plays without
    making a mistake,
      he continues to swim in the air,
        his fingers remembering
          Brahms, Mendelssohn, Rachmaninov,
          the last Romantics.

        Begin the beginning! he shouts
          the title of a Broadway tune,
            while he circles the earth,
              looking for a safe place to land.

He shines, they say, like a morning star,
   the living and the dead,
     down on their knees,
      reciting the first gospel, water,
       and the miracle is, he comes down—

        not on a bayonet,
         not in the country where stars extinguish,
         making holes for the largest choir on earth,
        not in the garden where his mother,
       with him inside her, lay humming,
      alive in her shallow grave,
     while soldiers marched overhead—

    but in the holy place
  where all our ancestors sleep.

n the womb. *O Welt ich muss dich lassen.* Oh world I must leave thee, a poem by Brahms playing in his head, his fingers touching the ivory teeth of martyrs making the

Mixing in grief

for James Hall

i

The road to Selkirk
winds through the lowlands of Scotland,
past the ruins of medieval towns
and killing fields filled with lambs,
where our ancestors, reiver bards and singers,
stole sheep from the English
and cut off their heads where they slept.
It follows a river full of spawning fish
and is lined with dry stane,
the stone fences without mortar
our grandfathers left
when they came to Canada.

my

My father's father from away
sang in the village kirk.
He had the voice of an angel,
they said. *Pannis angelicus.*
Everyone in the village was hungry,
but he left home with bread in his pocket,
scones or bannock his mother baked,
mixing in grief with the flour,
the morning he left, riding the rails
and a sailing ship to Paradise.

Later my grandfather married,
then crossed the Atlantic again,
marched to France in a skirt
with the Ladies from Hell
and sang for the enemy on holy days.

father's

ii

Now, two lifetimes away,
someone is singing "Silent Night"
in Spanish to the *torcedores*,
women rolling cigars on their thighs
at the factory Partagas in Havana.

I wonder if this is what my grandfather
tasted when he licked
the end of his Christmas smoke
in the muddy trenches at Ypres;
the scent of my grandmother's apron
or maybe, if he was lucky, the soft
bulge between her garters,
that place men dream about
when they are far from home.

Once a year, my grandfather married me,
when he took off the paper ring
with a picture, *la mujer en los Habanos*,
a smoking, bare-breasted woman,
so unlike his churchgoing wife,
and put it on my finger,
before he lit his Christmas cigar.

father

I wasn't allowed to kiss my grandfather.
He was gassed at Ypres,
sometime after he smoked the gift
sent all the way from home.
Even though he pissed in his kilt
and held it over his face,
his beautiful boy's lungs for singing
and chasing sheep over the green
hills of Scotland
filled up with blood.

iii

Gift, in German, means poison.
There are so many words in so many
languages for "Silent Night,"
but the tune is always the same.
When the German soldiers heard
my grandfather singing in the trenches
after he'd finished tasting
my grandmother's apron,
the turkey dinner he was imagining,
they came over no man's land
with a white flag
and asked him to sing for them.
Afterward, they shook hands
then returned to their holes in the ground.

It was quiet all that starry
night in France while the silent
gas crept into my grandfather's
sleep; where a naked
woman was rolling cigars on her thigh,
the Paradise he was dying for.

from

awaY

T H I S is where you come in

for M. K.

When your grandmother's
grandmother left her lonely
garden under the sea,
hungry for two-legged men
and the chance to make
angels in the snow,
she was so smart.

She stood on dry land
and anointed herself with water.
She invented religion and boats,
then sent her children to discover
the world was round, not flat,
and full of holes to fall into.

This is where you come in, and prayer.

You got down on your hands and knees,
the way she crawled out of the ocean,
sprouting fingers and toes,
the things you looked for first
when your children were born,
while snow fell around you,
your hair and eyebrows turned white,
and the surface of the lake froze hard:

you begged your child
to move his lips under the ice,
the way your grandmother's grandmother did
when she thought about climbing the stairs,
and never imagined that you
would have to come down
from the top of the mountain
and circle the lake with his black dog,
who will not eat or leave,
dragging your wrinkled breasts in the snow,
hoping for a miracle like the one
that made him gasp and breathe
like the first fish out of water
the day he entered the circle
of light surrounded by laughing
ravens, and he did.

voodoo queen

My granddaughter likes the blues.
She's the Voodoo Queen tonight,
a boogie chile tripping in a swanky
pink dress, eight sizes too big
with red balloons in the bosoms
and rhinestones around the hem.

       She's a good rockin' mama,
       holding her baby tight in her arms
       as she turns and turns,
       dancing in the path of dangerous
       candles her skirt barely misses.

She holds baby in her lap
while we sit by the fire drinking
something red for Valentine's Day
to match the heart-shaped cookies
the Voodoo Queen iced herself
and sprinkled with candies.

       She's a heart breaker,
       a hard-headed woman of four.
       The baby is naked,
       her rubber bum exposed and cold.

I am the pretty one, she says,
jealous of her own,
the royal female prerogative,
high on her throne,
a place we both like to visit,

but she holds baby close to her red
bosoms and prays out loud,
louder than John Lee Hooker
frailing on the radio,
Dear God, listen to me!
Don't let my baby
fall in the deep alligator swamp.

I close my eyes and imagine
alligators with clocks in their stomachs
ticking away in the shallow water,
waiting for rubber babies
and little girls in swanky dresses
to grow up and lose their balance.

The alligators are thirsty.
She pours the red drink,
a mixture of berries, her elixir d'amour,
into tiny white china teacups.
Keep your hands to yourself,
on the radio, John Lee Hooker
takes a bite of my heart
just as my granddaughter
sinks her teeth in a Valentine cookie,
staining her mouth and her tongue.

It's just pretend, she says,
popping the red ballOOns.

p e r f e c t   f e e t

In the herb garden,
the sick children sit in a circle.
None of them move.
She is wearing her new
lavender dress with sparkles.
She picks sprigs of real lavender,
holds them before their expressionless
faces and orders, *Smell!*
Her sun is high in the sky.
She has a magic wand and a party dress.
Alakazaam! Bippity, boppity, boo!
Her sparkles dance like stars on water.

Her father is playing his trumpet,
a song for running horses.
A few children notice.
They move their hands.
Some of them open their eyes.

She takes off her shoes,
runs, runs, as fast as she can,
away from the plastic bags with warnings
and drownings in lakes and rivers,
wherever the other children have been.

Run, her father wishes,
his heart bursting,
his lips blowing harder
than wind bending grass.
Run as fast as you can
on your perfect feet.

This is what he sees
beyond the rows of fragrant herbs
and children who have been
to the bottom of the sea.
Her hair flies.
    Her dress flies.
        Her feet fly.

He should save some breath
for wishing on dandelions gone to seed.
This is the moment before
they both discover the broken glass.

following
the
shape

Your Japanese comb, an *omba*,
is a lacquer stick with holes
and metal teeth that slide back and forth.
Here, they call it a contour gauge.
You used it for slumping glass,
the comb following the shape
and shaping itself,
told us your daughter liked to play with it.
It made me think of that toy we had,
with nails that fell into a box
accepting the form of a nose or hand,
the surprises I found
after the children went to bed.
You were selling it, you said,
because the comb was stuck
and the memory painful.
You talked about broken glass
the day she left with your child,
both of them wearing sundresses
with the straps crossed in the back.

You described them then,
making a cross with your hand,
the **X** and the **X** walking away
into the morning,
their matching shoulders,
the tans on their backs
the indelible **X** and **X** in their sleep
in some motel for mothers and daughters
halfway between here and there,
the child with her face sliced in half,
half you and half her,
the scab forming in a line,
down the forehead, over the nose
and the lips and the chin,
how you felt when you saw her,
thinking, *What have we done?*

Later, in your studio,
you heated the glass and found the comb
with the perfect line of her profile,
her blood in it still.

PALE KNOWLEDGE
PALE KNOWLEDGE
PALE KNOWLEDGE
PALE KNOWLEDGE
PALE KNOWLEDGE
PALE KNOWLEDGE
PALE KNOWLEDGE

pale knowledge

Pail nolish, she orders,
transposing the letters,
her baby fingers held out for paint.
It could be a prayer for the dead, in Hebrew,
or the name of a Russian river.
It could be invisible cities, beyond the Pale,
where children like her lost their dolls
between the legs of galloping horses.

She wants to wear the family pearls,
my high-heeled shoes,
a dress that sparkles.
She is Mrs. Queen at her tea parties,
eating her bread and honey
with all the crusts cut off.
She gossips on, does all the voices,
while her children sleep as long as she likes,
their little mouths painted shut.

These are our first ceremonies.
We do not take our daughters into the jungle
and circumcise them with rusty razors.
We do not bind their feet.
We do not sacrifice them in cenotes
ruled by miscreant gods.

Call me mother, she commands,
pouring watered-down tea
from my grandmother's silver pot.
She can already feel the tiny
lips tugging her nipples.

You want to hold the pose,
the veiled hat at an angle,
the lipstick smeared on her face.
You want to take this pale knowledge
and paint your door so the angel
of sex and death will pass over
with a sword in her arm saying

stop!

silver foil

A match strikes in the dark
and another silver
paper floats to the ground
in cities where lost children
lie in the same direction as snow.

A woman who gathers them every
morning and sells them to tourists
says they are sacred relics.
Burn marks on the foil
could be nails from the Garden
of Gethsemane, where white
flowers with opium seeds
grow out of the bodies of men.

She says they are beautiful
and you have to believe her,
just as the lost children
living on sidewalks all over the world
believe a sky full of babies in pale
dresses could land, just once,
with a prayer on them.

This is how the sky falls down on quiet
streets in London, Paris,
Havana, and the *Bario Gotico* in Barcelona,
where snow has the sound of mercy
and stoned children come out of the shadows,
take off their gloves and wait
for angels with trumpets and small feet
to march across their outstretched hands.

The woman who collects the silver
foil and trades them for food
for the hungry calls them
her veil of tears when the solstice
moon blossoms in fields of poppies
           and small addicts with their arms held out,
chasing the dragon, stand still as white
crosses in the middle of the road.

down into pAradise

She wants to be on top of the world.
Higher, she says, *higher!*
each time you lift her
or push the swing,
look up and see her silhouette
eclipse the morning light.

She wants to climb the ladder herself.
She wants to be Queen of the Castle.
She wants the power and the singing
thrill of sliding down into Paradise.

She is the summit—
Nefertiti in turquoise and gold,
The Red Queen in red shoes
running to the edge of a parquet floor
screaming *Off with his head,*
the Queen of England
riding the royal barge down the Thames
with her Mr. King to the grassy place
where a dark philosopher
sits in the sun drinking tea
that came from China,
savouring the taste of heresy.

She wants to be Jill up the hill,
Icarus's sister,
the little engine that could,
the first woman on Everest,
a feminist theologian
who dares to look at the brightest star
and lose her head.

No hat, she says, the sun in her eyes,
and lifts both hands off the ladder
then falls, head first,
the descent in slow motion,
taking forever, a movie rewinding,
a fist in your throat,
the sensation of drowning,
then lands in your arms,
safe as she can be.

CHILDREN OF PARADISE

Tonight we are floating in the numb
arms of the children of Paradise,
near the street where the homeless
have been told they must sleep standing up,
like those blinkered horses
who pull humans through
beautiful gardens with fountains
for money on hot summer days.

The street children hold out
their begging cups
with arms full of needles.
They open their mouths, gasping for air,
but they don't make a sound,
are quieter than coins in cups,
quiet as the water
babies at the bottom of the lake
full of swans and lilies,
where the angel of light
fell when he got mountain sickness,
as children do who stand for a moment
on the highest rock in the neighbourhood.

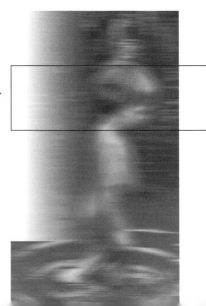

On the highest rock,
a child can be queen for a day,
can determine the sex of angels and airplanes,
is a god until someone pushes her off.

On this night, on the third rock from the sun,
the street children sleep standing up,
and you and I are naked as babies in water
held down by gravity.

Night bloomers yawn in the lake.
When we swim among them,
they take us in their arms
and their long hair wraps around our legs.
We can stay here forever,
because we have stood on high rocks too,
when all we could see was lakes
full of swans and water lilies
and children who bloom at night
because they are not allowed to lie down.

I also remember the sleeping part,
your daughters in our bed,
side by side on a silk comforter,
one with the marble face of a Renaissance
Madonna, her sister dark,
with the largest eyes in the world,
big enough for a nest of crows.
She said they flew out of her eyes,
and circled the small body of herself,
a comma in an oval of lashes so long
no one believes they are real.

The girls were so tangled,
their hair and their arms and legs,
they might have been drowning.
You said you went down to the ocean
in this dream you had in the hospital,
when they gave you opium for rest,
and you held your arms over the water,
waiting for love to arrive.

Perhaps you were waiting for them
    to rise to the surface one last time,
        these girls who look like the men

            who came to you on rafts

                from islands where men are sent

                    when the world no longer loves them.

Their fathers came like the ghosts of zebras,
horses in striped pyjamas,
your dark daughter would say,
their bodies branded by light
coming through prison bars.

Those were the cracks you slipped through
and sank and tasted the ocean,
fear on the skin of men
rowing, one at a time, for their lives.
Twice and this was the third time
you scooped the bottom of the sea,
your arms held like a spoon,
and what none of us wanted
or could help was a drowning,
girls wrapped in each other's hair,
their legs and arms frantic
in their mother's opium dream.

divorce monkey-style

If you believe everything you read,
monkeys have adjustable jaws.
When they are wrenched from their mates
by death or divorce monkey-style,
their embouchure changes.
Think of it; big lips, little lips
a different sound for every season of love.
This is the fanfare when monkey
lust trumpets through the forest,
notes as brassy and loud
as the arrival of Renaissance royalty,
when they swing from branch to branch
with the sound of little tin cups
full of the talking heads of kings
and queens in *mariages de convenance*
clutched in their prehensile hands.

Monkeys mate for life,
and so, they say, do humans.
All of us except for monks in their robes,
missing that last syllable, the key
that opens the door to heaven.
Monks have the mandate for prayer—
they have the technology,
organs and organ music—
while monkeys simply get to rejoice
in a canopy of singing birds,
mangoes and coconuts.

No wonder the children,
their mouths filled with milk
and the foreign language
spoken by their parents,
love the monkey songs and the monkey trees
that line the boulevards in our city.
No wonder they pinch each other
and wish when they see one.
No wonder their secret wishes
are the wishes of children all over the world:

Make them love each other.

You can read their non-adjustable
lips in the rear-view mirror.

except for one

Yesterday, someone was buried.
Limousines rolled by with their lights on,
tinted windows rolled up,
except for one, open a crack,
wide enough for the hands of a child,
his fingers ecstatic as puppies
riding into the wind.

For twenty years we rode in a hearse,
the windows closed.
We couldn't see out or in,
spent so much time in the dark,
now it is hard to remember your face.

Except in Venice, where the light was perfect.
The children ate ice cream all afternoon
and in the evening our son, the *piccolo cantore*,
sang in the piazza, filled his gondolier's hat
with coins he put under his pillow
so every time he moved we could hear it.
Tonight Venice, he said in his sleep,
his voice sounding like money,
Italian royalty arguing in bed,
tomorrow the world.

The next day, at the Lido,
a hairdresser put his hand on my breast.
Mi sciocco, he said. *Prego, mi scusi.*
We had lunch in the grand hotel
and rented a seaside cabana.
I remember making love in the wooden hut,
(even though you never did say *love*),
while the children played in the sand,
Italian sunlight slanting through vents
in the swinging door at the beach
where Mahler wrote that beautiful music,
Death in Venice, the death of our marriage,
our children's hands, thirty fingers
in a funeral cortège,
fluttering through the louvres.

indian time

I met Slater Bob on the last ferry to Saanich.
All the way across, we could see Christmas
lights shining in the harbour.
Slater was driving a beater with a stuck window,
his sister's car—she let him take it to the Shaker
House because maybe a prayer would fix it.
Slater is big and a lay preacher now
and he said the cold didn't bother him much.
I always wondered about that,
how Indian kids could stand in the river
full of mountain snow without shivering,
how they never wore jackets, even at Christmas.

I asked if his mother still carded her wool,
if the sign was still up on Tussie Road,
banning honkies like me from the Rez,
who came in the night to steal children,
especially boys like Clyde,
whose mother died in the car one Christmas Eve
when she was too drunk to get out
with the baby who made it to morning.

Clyde grew up wild, loving the river,
knew every elusive salmon by name,
loved his freedom, and was loved by me,
even when things turned bad,
when he phoned from jail
and asked me for paints and paper,
so he could make pictures
the way we did when he was a child.

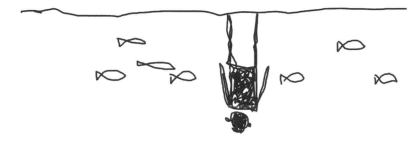

It was so lonely in jail, he said,
but one of the inmates was building a sweat lodge
and he would be out before long
riding the wind or a stolen car.

Slater was going to a prayer meeting
and my husband and I were avoiding
an accident on the highway.
We could hear carols across the water.
Slater's hearing is better than mine.
When I looked at his lips, I could read them.
He was telling me something, not
the words to the song, but something
that happened in Indian time.
Somewhere along the road to Christmas
and the last ferry from Cowichan to Saanich,
my watch must have stopped for the moment
Clyde stepped inside,
put the gun in his mouth and fired.

MONTEGO BAY

In Montego Bay, where tourist
families are happy playing pirate
and riding down waterfalls,
the barrel kids live in shacks
with photos of their mothers with other children
stuck in mirrors otherwise used
in voodoo ceremonies involving whisky and smoke,
things my own father smelled of
when he bent over to kiss me goodnight.

Today I caught a glimpse of my face
in a window and saw him for the first time.
Both of us were surprised, as if we were looking
down opposite ends of a telescope.
No one would look away first.
It's an old game children play
when they are trying to kill one another.
This is the stranger the barrel kids see
when they look through the whisky and smoke
at black women with faces like theirs,
smiling at white kids surrounded by snow.

These photographs come in cardboard
barrels filled with food,
hand-me-down clothes
and letters that say, *Someday*
you'll come and we'll be together
when I've saved enough money. Love

Mother—

a word that tastes like cardboard,
not the soft fle**sh they try to remember at night,**
in bed with three other cousins,
bedbugs sipping their blood, slowly, as if it were rum,
and can't when they finally meet at the airport,
mother and child, face to face—
not even later,

say it.

child of the revolution

Lila sits high as a hybrid
queen on her little suitcase
in the back seat of Abelardo's blue
pre-revolution Dodge,
which needs several repairs
during the journey home from La Boca,
mouth in the hungry language of Spain.
She is eating mandarinas,
throwing the skins out the window
for road-grazing pigs, the fine
gold hair on their bodies the precious
metal at the end of the rainbow
arching over the aching
jungles of Oriente province,
where poets have died for girls like her.

It has been raining in the Oriente.
A hurricane has brought water
and death after two years of drought.

Abelardo is a *caballero* in the car
bought by his father before the Yankee
blockade that will never starve Cuba,
even though children are dying.
He drives slowly around holes in the road,
careful not to bruise his passenger
or the precious black market fish
bought from *hombres* at *la playa*,
where the sea is so blue it hurts to look,
bluer than the *ojos azul* of the mulatto
poet at the fiesta in Holguin,
where children threw flowers in the river
on the day the hero, Jose Marti, died on the beach,
bluer than the music my husband played

with the Santeria band at the Casa de la Trova,
bluer than bruises on the arms and legs
of the blind woman we saw on the street,
cupping her hand like a begging bowl.

I want your blue eyes, the young
prostitute Armando hired with our rent
the night his wife went to the hospital
told me as easily as Lila's mother
asked for my hat the day we left Holguin,
as if some small adjustment might make
these *mujeres* into royalty too.

You are my blue-eyed máquina de la mar,
said Lila, child of the revolution,
riding my back into the blue Caribbean,
digging her heels in my sides.

Whale, in Spanish, is *ballena,*
the word so close to ballerina; this is
what Lila becomes when she closes her eyes
and spins on the marble
floor of her ruined mansion in Holguin,
transforming this northern visitor
into violin bows, oil for cooking,
needles for sewing the string dresses
women sell on the street to tourists
and fat for soap to wash the family laundry
so long as it rains on the old blue
Dodge she rides like a queen
through the drought-starved jungle
where the revolution began
when Abelardo's blue
taxi was just a baby too.

SONG OF AFRICA

Angelina Zwane was born in a cinderblock
shack without running water or electricity,
but she was loved by her mother and father
and her cousin Francina Diamini,
who carried her everywhere.
They said Angelina floated
in her white baby dress.

Her feet never touched the ground.

Every morning, when the equatorial
sun trumpeted over the fields,
dung beetles drove their children
to water in compost chariots,
elephants held theirs aloft in ivory teeth,
and Francina, with Angelina in her arms,
sailed through grass singing
the song of Africa,
giraffes, zebras, and antelopes,
taking their babies to the river
to drink because it was holy water
that should have belonged to every
creature that wandered the plain.

In the far country, where tigers sometimes
chase each other until they are butter
and black children become
rivers flowing across the veld,
crying freedom, the African hymn,
everything melts into one note,
the grey of elephant grief and chanting
kaffirs circling a tiny
coffin covered in white chrysanthemums.

This is the song of Angelina Zwane,
whose feet never touched the ground,
not even when her cousin
Francina was shot in the back,
carrying her to water.

LOS Curiosidade da BAHIA

The voodoo woman lit a cigar
and blew the smoke in her mirror.
That was the first time I saw you,
standing up straight in the window
that used to appear in a dragon's breath,
when people believed in such things
and fairy tales were written
for girls with long hair
crimped in the shape of their plaits.
The cigar was twisted and she told me
some were braided, one to the other,
marked for tobacco workers
so they couldn't sell them or give them away.

The *cigarrilhas da Bahia*
are shaped like the legs of children
deliberately crippled,
who beg in the streets of Brazil
while their mothers paint angels,
each of them carrying the name
of a child to protect.

It happens like this all over the world;
rivers that lick crooked
paths around mountains,
back to the sea or the tiny
feet of concubines folded in half
so they stay with their men
in the opium dens of China.

When we were children, they made us
sit up straight in our chairs
and walk with metal coat hangers
pressed against our shoulders.
This is how we grew up
until love transformed us,
husbands and wives discovered in smoking
mirrors clarified by nightshade,
braided in years of pleasant conjugal sleep,
until we too were properly aged
and bent to the shape of each other.

city of miracles

City of Miracles

Comforter, where, where is your comforting?

— Gerard Manley Hopkins

ADAGIO in G minor

It is almost always a miracle
when hungry people line up for bread
and, while the line moves slowly,
adagio in the language of music,
angels tune up their voices
and the bread divides.

This was the sound in the sky
when the people of Sarajevo
waited that morning, their stomachs
rumbling almost as loud
as gunfire in the marketplace.

We have a name for it, *agoraphobia*,
fear of the sky and the place
where fruit and vegetables are sold
and sometimes women and children
lined up for bread are scattered
among the loaves and fishes
and baskets of oranges,
their hands and feet
measured in pounds and ounces.

No wonder Smailovic, the cellist,
trembled as he dressed
in his white tie and tails,
no wonder the Adagio in G Minor
had so much vibrato.
For twenty-two days, for twenty-two souls,
and then for twenty-two months,
while the bombs fell around him,
Smailovic sat in the ruined
onions and potatoes,
the smashed melons,
the ghosts of his neighbours, and played,
every note for someone who died
in the lineup for bread.

Wicked messenger

In the park, children feed bread to the swans
     and ducks—the sign in the grass
          says THE SWANS BITE, but they don't.
          By the road that runs through the park,
               a demented woman stands on the curb
                    with her own bag of crumbs
                    which she throws on the street,
                         hoping the birds will think the street is a river
                    and the birds will fall under the cars.

          In the urban mythology of this city,
               there is the story of a cruel man
          who fills a sack with singing birds each evening
               and clubs them until they are quiet.

               A bird in the house, they say, means death.
                    They say *Kill the messengers*,
                         millions of birds with holes in their chests
                         served up in *cuisine minceur*
                              on fine china plates dribbled with puréed
                         vegetables the colour of avian blood.
                         Bite the bullet, they say,
                              sons and daughters of Eli, the priest at Shiloh,
                         bullets hidden so well in the flesh
                    you might swallow them when
                    you swallow the notes of a bird
               breaking the sound barrier.

Under the ground, where precious metals lie
sleeping with the bones of our ancestors,
what miners fear most is the moment
the caged canaries stop singing.

In my dreams, I can sail through the air
        like a voodoo queen or Eli, the prophet,
              his holy messages in his hand.
              There is a h   O   le in my chest

              so big you can see those birds falling out of the sky.

p e r n k o p f

My grandmother was the last one
in her family to leave Vienna,
a city famous for music,
especially the romantic composers,
Schubert and Strauss, their lyrics
as graceful as Viennese streets,
fine-boned women and the waltz,
lovers in the late afternoon,
when the light is perfect,
dancing in a famous cafe.

What the Viennese artist,
who knew Schubert's lieder by heart,
the word itself meaning "love song,"
read with his heart was not the silk
folds of a dress circling the dance floor
or the line of a breast or an ankle,
or the hollow at the base of a woman's neck,
where desire has the lustrous shape of a pearl,
but the lines of music beneath the skin,
where the heart and the brain
are connected by ribbons of blood.

Pernkopf was a perfectionist,
every dissection exquisite,
the skin of an abdomen folded back
revealing the child within,
a grey pearl, uncircumcised,
unborn, you might say the child of Plato,
his body the signature of God,
and his mother, bathed in formaldehyde,
one of those human women who had coffee
and pastry and fell in love
in a café with string quartets.

Now fifty years later, a doctor,
who also loves Schubert and his own wife
and the idea of human perfection,
turns the pages in the book by Pernkopf,
the Viennese anatomist,
and what he sees in veins and arteries
is not music but the strangled
roots of murdered families
and the artist's signature, not of God
or anything Holy, but men
who charged their brushes
with the blood of Viennese Jews.

go mad

In Japan, the homeless

monkeys go mad as apartment cats

with no dirt for burying their waste.

There are no blue bottoms advertising sex

where monkeys wearing pants

stolen from clotheslines

swing between balconies

in a home forest of windows and stairs.

There are no monkey babies

for tourists with cameras to photograph,

where underwear with the erotic

smells of adolescent girls

is sold in vending machines

and old ladies, deprived of estrogen,

sit on public benches

nursing dolls with human lips,

their tired breasts exposed.

At least they could iron them,

someone from the civilized world,

where male monkeys on hormones

have durable erections, observed

the day Roy Rogers died and should have been

stuffed and mounted on Trigger,

while primates, mad as apartment cats

with no dirt for burying their waste,

were climbing fire escapes

in the urban forests of Japan

looking for a quiet place to nurse

kittens they stole from

the arms of Japanese children

while their grandmothers, raised in paper

houses burned in the fires of Nagasaki

and Hiroshima, looked the other way.

mad apples

i

Don't eat tomatoes, my grandmother said.
She told me they were mad apples
and the seeds were poisonous,
excreted by men who crossed the Andes,
tasted the fruit and, filled with lust,
ran naked into the ocean,
rode warm-blooded mammals
all the way home to Europe,
where princes of the church
went blind with desire,
and fallen women were still wearing red.

The king's mistress sold them at Covent Garden,
aphrodisiac fruit shaped like a heart,
rotten ones thrown at the orchestra and fat sopranos.
Would the musicians play better, sing better
bathed in the jism of an unrepentant plant?
Xtomatl, wolf peach, loved by Cortez
and Marco Polo, hated by Puritans,
roundheads, the perfect ingredient
for a perfect silence, *le petit mort,*
when pleasure was a mortal sin.
They found them stuffed in the mouths
of men who died with erections
and in the mad Maharanee's fainting cocktail,
puréed with ground diamonds,
at the end of the Raj,
when nervous high-born women in India,
descended from gods, read backwards
and began fucking their dogs.

When my grandmother spoke,
    my mouth felt dry.
        I was planted in sand.

        This is how dogwood
      came to live in the desert.
      Dogwood, the true cross.
       On the third day,
    the dogs came down from the trees
       where dogs started out,
    their breath smelling like the first
      garden where the first
  man and woman lay down to eat
and, when they bit into the skin,
      it was delicious.

   They loved eating the love apple.
    Never say love when it's food,
my grandmother said, *it is vulgar,* her dog
   sniffing her skirt while she prayed.

She gave me a holy white organdy dress,
   which I wore inside out for good luck,
  and the book with backwards words.
Dog is love, I read, and her dog jumped up,
    hearing his name called out.
His paws were muddy, red as tomatoes.
    He'd been running to meet me
   through the fields of the Lord
   where mad apples grow wild.

ii

In a crack between the first
        and second millennia, now,
        while miracles are still possible,
      a little girl in a white dress
     takes a kitchen knife
    and cuts a ripe tomato in half.
   She finds in the crimson
  seeds and veins a message from God
written in Aramaic script.

       This happens in London,
       not far from the tower
       where scholars read sacred books
       and *muezzin* sing out the time.

They come to the girl's house
and read the tomato, which says,
There is only one God.

     An acrobat hanging from a tree
      in an enchanted forest in Germany
      hears the holy men translate
       the ancient language of peace,
        comes down and begins to set
       all the stones in the world on end.

He balances stone on stone,
some of them striped with precious metal,
gold and fool's gold,
some of them shaped like men
and women and children.

You can almost see air
   between rocks so fragile
      wind knocks them over, and music,
        afternoon ragas, sun chasing sun
    over the sound of water on stones,
        the bodies of believers
          in holy rivers
       floating toward the sun,
     stones rolling end over end
      and children on leashes,
anxious as wishes, dodging the stones,
      pulling the men and women
        back to the garden
   where they begin picking stones
       and circling the garden
     until thcy too fall down
     and turn into stone.

Here is an acrobat balancing stones.

Here is a child in her white dress,
    the organdy bodice stained
      with juice from a tomato
      inscribed with ancient text,
        holding her breath,
      willing the rocks that are
        still to stay still.

I remember the splash of you
hitting the ground
when you fell from the hayloft
and the beautiful inside of your brain,
a sunset, when they put it back
the way it kept ticking,
like all those clocks in our house.

We are superstitious,
wind the clocks every Tuesday,
never let them run down.
This is the first fact of life—
the clocks must keep ticking.
You say it is madness,
and you are not mad.
You fell when everyone was watching.

The mad woman in rags
vanished between then and now,
the day we turned our clocks
        back to standard time.
                You were walking down the street
                    while she was climbing the stairs.
                        They said she was crazy,
                            but she had a genius for timing.

                        They said she was breathtaking
                        once, out of this world,
                        a Paris model walking on air.

                    We were all winding our watches,
                    but not you—you looked up,
                even though you'd been told a thousand times
never to stare at the sun.

You said it went dark for a moment.
  She covered up the sky.
  Then she stretched out,
  a bird of paradise, every
  couturier's dream.

  You thought you heard a pumpkin smashing.
 Then you heard clocks ticking again.
    But it wasn't clocks at all—
it was two hungry crows
pecking her brain on the pavement.

When you woke at midnight
and told me about your dream,
you said you'd been making love to a melon.
In your sleep, you smelled a cantaloupe
ripening on the window sill
and thought it was me.

e n t e r i n g   t h e   m e l o n

Then I dreamed you died inside a muskmelon,
and the room we were sleeping in
turned orange, the colour of prayer
and holy rivers in India.
Even the window was gold and the dead
fingers that tapped on the glass as they passed.
I could smell the garbage and the bodies,
marigolds floating to Nirvana
where the human spirit is free.
You were lost in the garbage and the flowers
and the only way to find you again
was to follow my nose, the way moths
smell their way back to the garden
in storms of blossoms the colour of cantaloupe.

I dreamed your spirit
   walked over a carpet of marigolds
     and I was mad to smell
       the soles of your feet.

        What if I walk in my sleep
         while you are dreaming of melons,
          opening the ripe flesh with your hands
           entering seeds warmed by the sun,
           and go into the bed of a man
           who picks marigolds
           and weaves them into blankets
           that float dead Buddhists to bliss?

        What if I come back to your bed
         smelling as if I've been rolling in marigolds
        and you find me there, in your arms, in the
        morning,
       perhaps dead, no time for explanations
      this side of the grave,
     one of his fingers in my mouth,
   as if they were toes, your toes, remember,
scented with petals from my dream?

the joshua tree

In the dream, your mouth was full of sand.
You were crossing the desert
when you saw the bones of a woman
hanging from a Joshua tree.
It was beautiful, her bones
banging together inside her dress.
Or was there a man with a stick?
You weren't sure.
It was night and the tree
was surrounded by blinding light.

Someone is dying, you said,
that long-ago time,
the moment an epiphany,
when you ran from your parents' room,
your nightgown flying,
revealing the moonlit shape of a girl
shaped like a succulent
tree full of candles
and holy cannibals eating each other,
hanging their luminous
bones from the branches.

The woman in the tree was smiling,
her lips painted with a brush.
She had swallowed her shoes
and climbed the tree herself.
Perhaps she was hungry,
aroused by the sound of beaks and jaws,
creatures performing their small
ceremonies for sex and death.
Perhaps she lit the candles herself.
Her hair was on fire
and maybe she knew
you were coming to save her.

WE ARE BURIED TO THE WAIST. YOU SAY *DROWNING*, MAKING WAVES IN THE SNOW WITH YOUR BARE ARMS. WE WERE SITTING IN THE BATH WATCHING CHILDREN SLIDE DOWN THE HILL ON OLD CARPETS AND A BOY IN A BOAT IN THE LAKE AT THE BOTTOM OF THE HILL. WE DREW ON THE WINDOW. MOTHER, YOU WROTE, FRONTWARDS AND BACKWARDS SO THE CHILDREN COULD READ IT TOO, BUT PROBABLY NOT. PROBABLY THEY HAVE BEEN TOLD NOT TO LOOK IN OUR WINDOWS. THERE IS TOO MUCH JOY IN OUR HOUSE FOR THE AVERAGE PERSON. IT'S LIKE LOOKING AT THE SUN. YOU NEED DARK GLASSES OR WOODEN SHADES WITH SLITS OR PERFORATED CARDBOARD. SOMEONE TOLD ME YOU COULD GET HIGH LOOKING AT THE SUN THROUGH THOSE TINY HOLES. THEY DO IT IN PRISON, ALL THE TIME, ANOTHER APOCRYPHAL STORY. THERE IS A HEADLESS WOMAN IN OUR GARDEN. HER METAL BREASTS POINT TO THE HOUSE. THAT IS SO THE CHILDREN IN THE PARK WON'T SEE. ONE OF THEM MIGHT STEAL HER. OR TELL. THE BREAST POLICE MIGHT COME. WE'VE ALREADY HAD THE PLAYING-TRUMPET-AFTER-NINE-P.M. POLICE AND THE SKYLIGHT-WITHOUT-A-PERMIT POLICE. NOW THAT WINTER'S HERE AND THE GARDEN LADY IS BURIED IN SNOW, UP TO HER NIPPLES, SURELY THE BREAST POLICE CAN'T BE FAR

BEHIND. MY MOTHER USED TO SAY YOU COULD DROWN IN A TEACUP. I THINK SHE HAD FRIENDS WHO DID. THEY KEPT THEIR GIN BEHIND THE TOILET. WHEN ONE OF HER FRIENDS WENT MAD, SHE PUT ON HER WEDDING DRESS, STUCK A NEEDLE FULL OF COUGH SYRUP IN HER ARM, AND SWAM OUT TO SEA. I USED TO DREAM ABOUT SAVING HER. SHE WOULD BE GRATEFUL. I WANTED SOMEONE TO NEED ME THEN. DREAMS ARE LIKE THAT. YOU NEVER GET THERE. NOT UNTIL YOU WAKE UP IN THE BATH WITH A MAN WHO CAN THINK FRONTWARDS AND BACKWARDS. WE RAN FROM THE BATH TO THE GARDEN. THE SNOW IS DEEP. WE ARE BURIED TO THE WAIST. YOU MISS ME ALREADY. YOU WANT A KISS. BECAUSE YOUR MOTHER SAID SHE WAS SWIMMING TO CHINA WHEN SHE WAVED BYE-BYE AND ONLY GOT TO THE FLOAT OUT WHERE IT WAS OVER YOUR HEAD AND YOU NEVER LEARNED TO SWIM, BECAUSE THE BOY IN THE DINGHY STILL HASN'T REACHED THE OTHER SIDE OF THE LAKE, BECAUSE THE MAN NEXT DOOR WHO WAS THE ONE WHO PHONED THE TRUMPET-AFTER-NINE-P.M. POLICE AND THE SKYLIGHT-WITHOUT-A-PERMIT POLICE KEEPS SHOVELLING SNOW, BECAUSE HE THINKS THE SKY IS FALLING AND HE MIGHT BE RIGHT, I SAY YES.

dancing with picasso

When I began dancing with the Cuban
    artist we called Picasso,
        even though the equatorial night
            was warm and he unbuttoned his shirt
        so I could feel his body
    hair was soft as swansdown,
you said you were not jealous.

You played fast, *allegro*, and I said
    I could keep on flying with Picasso
        until I saw heaven or the sun rise
            over the ancient city of Holguin,
            whichever happened first.
        You were making love to your mandolin
    and I was not jealous either,
because Picasso was lighter than air.

His real name was Angel, pronounced
    "On hell" in Spanish, but when I told you
        he returned from the dead
            the way they say homeless
                children rise like ghosts
            from the sewers of Moscow
        to hunt in the streets until morning
    when they vanish again,
you stopped the music.

I don't know why you did that.
I love the story you told me
about the widower who made a banjo
head from the skin of his wife's
thigh after she died.
Angel would say *culo*,
a shorter word with some of the same
letters as the word, in Spanish, for heart.

How easily one thing becomes another.

I told you angels have many shapes.
I've been waiting to dance with Picasso
and the hungry orphans who rise
like white smoke from the sewers
and take prisoners for their unholy
Eucharist under the ground.

They say the lost children
dismember their hostages and eat them,
and I say death is only a word,
just like the name "On hell,"
some white feathers,
or a pomegranate seed in my mouth,
and there is nothing between us but air,
the smell of lotus water from a lady's bath—
but you smell burning flesh,
the sewers of Moscow,
and now you tell me the genius
who transforms himself was a man
who burned his wife with cigarettes
the night she went dancing without him.

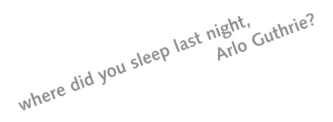

The war is over and our peaches ripen
faster than we can eat them.
It took that many years
for the tree to grow and Arlo's hair,
turning white in the garden
where his father wrote that last
desperate song in a folding chair—
Oh God, oh God, oh God—
words and music by Woody Guthrie.

This is the season of shooting stars,
when a boy took my married
mother for a last ride in his convertible
to look at the stars
and tell her he loved her once
before he went to sleep with the fishes
off a beach in Normandy.

I had my first kiss in the dark,
with horses grazing nearby,
from a boy whose name I forget
even though I can name the stars,
while the stars and stripes exploded
over the ancient cities of Indochina.

It was hot last night.
We took the ferry to Salt Spring
and had dinner in the shade of your fig tree,
salad with lamb from your fields
and wine from the holy vineyards of France.

At Arlo's concert, a girl with slender arms
offered to fan our faces for a nickel.
You can't buy much for a nickel now.
It's the price of a church candle
and the jukebox at Alice's Restaurant.
Someone brought an electric fan for Arlo,
his biggest fan, my husband said,
and everyone laughed, even the AWOL
American soldier with a fatal blood disease,
and Arlo's hair was blowing in the wind.

This is the song that altered history,
Arlo told us, eighteen minutes into the story
erased from the Watergate tapes,
because his gentle father,
his memory collapsed in a folding chair,
wrote one for the road to show him
poets can change the world.

Oh God, oh God, oh God.
Last night, the sky was a river of stars
flowing to the heart of the universe.

Where is Arlo sleeping tonight?
someone asked,
when Arlo's bus pulled out
and he began to circle the island
surrounded by sleeping fish,
his hair turning white in the moonlight,
singing the words to his father's last song
for all the nearly extinct species,
the soldiers and the marmots
and the girls with slender arms.

On the way to bed, we noticed
the green Spanish moss
hanging from your hawthorn tree
could be the beards of prophets,
marble by Michelangelo,
turning to dust in the garden
where Arlo prays with his father
and all the boys my mother knew
sleep with fishes gasping for air,
where the AWOL American soldier,
a hippy with a fatal blood disease,
got up to dance when Arlo sang
his father's song, *Oh God,*
oh God, oh God, because he could.

carr**i**ed away

for Francis Wilgress

My grandfather died in my bed
on a snowy afternoon.
We found him with the radio on
and a little *woody.*
That's what my brothers called them—
what you got in your sleep
when dreams were hunger and desire—
what happened to the mongoloid boy we saw
when he came into that dream restaurant
in Anaheim, California and saw
watermelons, strawberries, and bananas,
carried on the backs of angels
carved in ice, to heaven,
where boys get to eat what they like.

Woody was pleasure, the old station wagon
my grandfather drove to the beach
where we swam until we had goosebumps,
then ate fried potatoes,
with salt and vinegar, wrapped in newspaper.

Woody was the sound of a clarinet
played by an idiot savant,
who lay in bed every day
listening to the radio lady
who lived in the old Marconi

banging his spoon on the rails,

       and glasses of water,

              and the steam radiator,

until someone noticed he was a genius too—
just like my grandfather
who ran his silver spoon around
the iron fence of his life,
stuttering, the sound of a train going somewhere
and the boy locked inside
the passionate body that lay in my bed
with the radio on and a woody
waiting for an angel carved in ice
to come and take him away.

City of miracles

There was an angel on the news last night.
She was washing the prostitutes' weary
feet and rubbing them with oil,
explaining that a girl's foot
gets down and dirty riding
bitch on a motorcycle.

They drag in the dirt.

She might be straddling a man
or a bike, the fender between her legs,
or sitting in a car with mud
splashing up through the floor,
or at the back of an Alabama bus
if her grandmother was one of those
who picked cotton and stopped to give birth,
her feet cracked and thirsty
as the fields she worked in.
She might be feeling the wind
in her face, like a dog
holding on for her life,
while the stranger,
wearing a helmet,
always gets to drive.

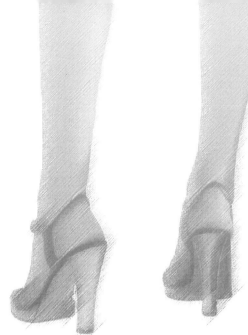

Keep your feet on the ground,
the angel said and she wasn't kidding.
The higher you are, the harder you fall.

Clowns wear stilts, and so did
Chinese ladies at court and Venetian
noblewomen teetering near canals
polluted by sewage and the damned
thrown off the Bridge of Sighs
in the middle of the night,
and so do the girls who work
on the corners downtown
every night of the week,
their shoes so high
only an acrobat could wear them.

The street children who ride
bitch for faceless drivers,
have dirty feet, their arches flat
and sore as the back of Ruth, the good
wife who threshed wheat in Biblical fields
and followed her husband to Paradise.

This is not the Promised Land, the angel said
as she rode a camera between the legs
of hookers in high-heeled shoes.
But it must be the city of miracles
when there is one angel who believes
God lives in the feet of a fallen
woman and washes them with her hair.

for Ed Mothersill

She has been to weddings.
Do they throw it at funerals too?
she asks in the restaurant
at the end of the breakwater,
where every item on the menu
ends on a bed of rice.
At night, she has rice dreams,
with cats and dogs and sheep
going round in circles
the way animals do
when they are about to lie down
to sleep or give birth to other animals
or be eaten in restaurants by children.

She is not sure she wants
to eat flesh any more.
She doesn't like it
when the peas touch the meat,
or when her parents tangle
their arms and legs in bed,
so she is forced to sleep between them.
She separates things on her plate.

At the pier, the day her friend died,
when she was afraid of the long
walk to the end of the ocean,
an angel came down from heaven
and gave her a shell to take home.
The angel was black and kind,
and held her hand for a moment.
She said he was a kindred spirit.

She called her scallop Jesse,
and he died too, but nobody ate him.
Jesse was buried in the garden
where her friend was the free spirit
who sat beside her on the bench
when she was playing with only one doll
and told her he'd rather
be himself and be alone
than join the crowd and be lonely.

He's being alone, she told her cousin
who said grief was a cat in his brain
that ate his curly red hair
when they were tying flowers
and childish drawings to the tree
her friend drove into the night
he took his eyes off the road,
and looked in the rear-view mirror for less
time than it would take a Chinese sage to write
the story of his life on a grain of rice.

window kissing

On the ride to the airport,
the girls are giggling in the back seat—
      kiss you, kiss you goodbye.
Would you kiss a lightbulb?
Would you kiss the dirty sidewalk?
Would you kiss the unthinkable,
grandfather with his beard
full of grey whiskers?
I kiss the window goodbye,
two little girls and a man with a beard,
easier to get into heaven,
according to scripture,
my lips on it for days, he told me later.
Just like his ancestors,
he kissed his fingers and touched them
every time he got into the car.

This is peace on earth,
the Yugoslav cab driver, used to war,
squints in the rear-view mirror.
Last week it snowed.
Today he is protecting his eyes from sunlight.

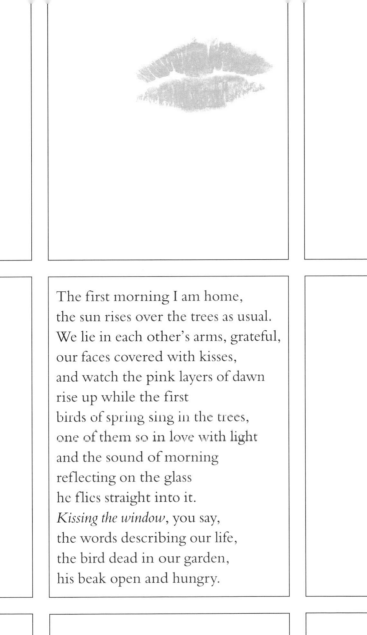

The first morning I am home,
the sun rises over the trees as usual.
We lie in each other's arms, grateful,
our faces covered with kisses,
and watch the pink layers of dawn
rise up while the first
birds of spring sing in the trees,
one of them so in love with light
and the sound of morning
reflecting on the glass
he flies straight into it.
Kissing the window, you say,
the words describing our life,
the bird dead in our garden,
his beak open and hungry.

the saning

The Saning

Though they go mad they shall be sane,
Though they sink through the sea they shall rise again.

— Dylan Thomas

the saning

This morning, we gargled water
before we left home to sing at the hospital
for children who lose their voices
in unimaginable accidents.
The crow in our pear tree,
as usual, adjusted her pitch
to that and every transient sound;
the newspaper landing on our porch,
a jogger dropping her water bottle in the park,
Johnny Mathis, the long-distance runner,
singing "Until the Twelfth of Never,"
his sostenuto amazing and lonely,
travelling to the end of the note,
the loneliness of the long-distance runner,
a film we remember from the time
I first fell in love with the sound of him

and my singing teacher,
who wore a jade ring and told us
his mother played music for the last Manchu
Empress on her island surrounded by lilies
and rare golden carp,
their songs audible to every child
who has walked on the bottom of the lake.

We were all dressed alike in my family
and for years I was singing
my way out of the wrong clothes.

For years, I loved men who loved men,
their enamel fingernails and brocade sleeves,
their falsetto voices—
Johnny Mathis, my singing teacher,
the boy I married—and sang like a crow,
from my throat, in my nest
full of bright shiny things,
three boy sopranos with perfect pitch,
until my throat refused.

This is your real voice, my husband said,
when I whispered *sotto voce* in bed
for him, and my black sister, the crow
vocalizing in the pear-laden
branch hanging over our house.
I have been looking for a comfortable
key for love and grief,
my pitch all over the place,
for the man who loves me and my children
and grandchildren and the children
I read about in the morning paper,
today three in New Mexico, suffocated in a trunk,
while their parents, who are cousins,
drove around listening to Johnny Mathis on the radio;
three in Ireland, sprinkled with holy water,
carried in tiny white coffins
from the country church near Ballymoney
after the Bishop of Down and Connor
blessed them and called them lambs of God
and the plaster Our Lady and St. Patrick
both looked away and wept.

It is a small miracle I am listening for—
the right key for statues weeping
and a bottle half full of water
caught before it lands on the path
in the park near our house;
my husband and I gargling in the morning,
when the crow gargles too, and we arrive
at the note at the end of our song
in the hospital for children
who lose their voices in unimaginable accidents
and one child from the silent
garden at the bottom of the sea,
who moves like a crab when her nurse
puts her down on the day-room floor,
sings with us, her pitch perfect.

carlo's gift

What does a woman keep in an evening bag
like the one Carlo has given me this time,
beads the colours of sunsets by Maxfield Parrish,
orange, magenta, amethyst,
silver putti at the clasp, Italian
angels with open mouths, singing
perhaps in some old square in Venezia,
Verona, after the opera, for change?

I ask my friend while we drink
Campari at Casa Fenestra
and he tells me about renting a room
from a Green Beret, who came back
from the Vietnam War with a gangrenous
hole in his thigh.
It's because of the bag, he said.
It was full of ears, you know. Trophies.
They cut off the ears of the dead.

The bag rubs and the hole never heals.

Now, none of us can sleep.
Not my friend, or my husband.
Not Carlo, who was an ophthalmologist
before he became a poet shopping for gifts
for other poets so they might write
poems about the gifts
which he will keep in a silver box,
the colour a slug excretes

when it enters the forest to mate,
or fight to the death,
eating the flesh of its mate, or its own.

Carlo might suggest eyes,
or the humours of the eye,
or even needles for pain.
Cats' eyes, perhaps, for seeing in the dark.
Maybe an eye with a needle through it,
which brings us back to the severed ears
and not to feminine things
such as combs and lipsticks, or even pearls.

My friend holds Carlo's evening
bag to my ear, and puts his finger to his lips.
When I listen, I hear angels
caterwauling in the filthy
canals of Europe and Indochina,
silver needles with eyes
working their way through holes
in semi-precious stones, the colours
orange, magenta, amethyst,
spelunkers singing underground,
in caves and graveyards and sewers,
for the ones who die when airplanes
spray for the gypsy moth, defoliating
the children, and the muttering of anxious
bulbs in the ground,
these poems rubbing my thigh.

a transparent apple

for Barbara Pedrick

It's an old dream.
The little girls are silent,
drowning their dolls in the sink
or leaving them out in the rain.
We hear variations on water
composers can't write down
between lines of music.

A transparent apple drops on the lawn.
It will bruise—these apples are delicate.
Are you having a poem? my husband asks,
his voice sleepy, the way he might say
Is your suitcase packed?
Are the little things ready?

This is not the dream part.
It is yesterday evening.
My friend and I are in the Cambodian
restaurant, and ginger tofu,
slices of grief, quiver on our forks.
My husband is playing music at a wedding.
Her husband is fiddling around
with a younger woman.

It is not the men we are missing tonight.

The phantom pain, the absolute
silence we're hearing,
is the sound of our children
born without making a sound,
the nights—it has to be night,
these things don't happen in daylight—
when we forgot to breathe for them.

My dreaming ends at sunrise
with the first cup of tea.
Another apple drops.
I want to catch it before it lands
and hold it safe.
Moon rocks, my husband says,
walking out of his sleep
into a sky full of apples,
their faces transparent.

I am writing my friend this
morning-after letter
to tell her the apples
are pale as our dead children,
but they never fall
so far from the tree we can't find them.

clear cut

The old man and his wife lie in the dark,
their heads resting on an axe,
listening to the convent garden,
trying to imagine the stairs to heaven,
the two of them dancing in top hat and tails,
her wedding dress and veil,
up the marble stairs to a shining
church made from the milk teeth of children
with beds to sleep in, where fairies found them
and left surprises under their pillows,
then kissed them goodnight, but never
touched them where children should not be touched.

The night is a forest, where lost children,
arms full of dirty needles,
sleep with their eyes wide open.
What the old man and his wife hear
is not the crack dreams of the homeless
drifting through condoms and syringes
but trees, planted by nuns, crying out.
The man and his wife are afraid to sleep,
in case the shining church they imagined
might be another convent surrounded by trees
littered with the dispossessed.

At midnight, the blade between them
divides the time between *then* and *now*,
making the moment the man goes mad
and enters with the axe in his hands.
He chops and the trees bleed while his wife
watches from the window.

In the morning, the trees are silent,
the songbirds gone from their branches.
The old man and his wife

watch legions of lost children,

faces pale as holy ghosts

multiplying in the dark

and feet accustomed to broken glass,

march out of the clear cut,

eyes adjusting to the light.

the circular lamp

In the painting, it is night.
The room, all curves, is lit from the window.
The woman sits on the bed half naked,
her hand resting on the man
curled in the quilt, like a child,
her foot hovering over the circular rug.
It could be a planet
she's spinning with her foot.
It could be a moon.
The surround is black, perhaps a wooden floor,
perhaps the cold and soundless space between them.
The man is not asleep.
He appears to be cold, maybe ill.
They both look straight at the artist.
Her brush is charged.
What happens next? is how they look at her.
What will it be tonight, life or death?

Are they about to make love?
    Will he throw off the quilt and ask her in?
    Will they rub together, making fire,
       the way their ancestors learned to warm
        those winter nights in the caves?
         The painter has painted her yellow
         and blurred her breasts.
         Will he find a nipple in the dark and suck?
      Will she cradle him in her arms
   and rock him to sleep?
Will they both slip off the bed and orbit the rug,
another moon for this evening
lit by the circular lamp on the porch?

forgetting was young

My mother is starting to forget
the secrets passed from woman to woman,
stories from before, boats hauled up,
scraping over rocks and barnacles,
hard to walk on, so we felt the cruel
sound of waves breaking in shells
the shape and colour of infant ears.

There was one she buried at the beach,
in a castle decorated with glass,
sand in her white satin shoes,
when the world she is now
forgetting was young.

Now her blood feels like sand.
The details of sand move through her,
telling the time, counting the faces
that surface in the same anxious wait
as for lost children, who come up
at last from the sea for air.

Last night, in the dark, my mother
went fishing for the man she married
before she discovered the salty
taste of women asleep in the tide.

She couldn't grasp it,
her hands frantic, cupping the water,
as bodies swam through the dark,
the dead floating upside down,
their faces unrecognizable,
their voices drowning at sea.

Red sky at night, they say,
is a sailor's delight,
but my mother couldn't sleep.
Her sheets smelled like sails.
Fish slipped through her net.

Then came the hook,
something old cast in the brass
flourish of sunrise,
wedding cake under her pillow,
silver print on a paper napkin,
a child conceived at sea,
the memory surprised in its sleep,
and the note by note
silver egress of fish
swimming through grey layers of dawn,
my father's name.

don sergio's feet

I imagine a painting by El Greco,
all light and dark.
All we can see in this frame
of the thick Ecuadorian night
is a flame in the corner,
Don Sergio's feet near the fire,
a can full of sticks
borrowed from the jungles of the Oriente.
Don Sergio's feet are dirty.
This peasant has never owned a pair of shoes.

    Don Sergio is playing a guitar
    carved from a single piece of wood.
    His songs are his own, the story of a slave,
    free at last, driving his homemade car
    from the *Costa* up to the high *Sierra*,
    all the way to the sky,
    where he will dance barefoot
    again with his brothers,
    the brass band from Cotopaxi.

I love you more than beans and rice,
he sings, because music is food to him,
because his heart is large enough
for the thin mountain air.

Don Sergio's wooden car has
third-generation tires made of sandals
recycled from *los autos de los ricos*.
The engine runs like a toy,
so graceful in traffic;
drivers of buses full of people
and chickens and holy medals honk because
they believe they are seeing a miracle,
maybe even a saint.

Even when he was a slave,
Don Sergio Henrique Spinoza—
his name inherited from the atheist
philosopher thrown out of Dutch synagogues—
danced to his own beat.

In Ecuador, money is sweet,
sucre, a name for sugar.
Sugar rolls off Don Sergio's tongue.
The people of Ecuador line the roads
to trade bananas and *dulces*, gas for the car
in exchange for Don Sergio's poems.
They call him *the poet in the dream car.*
Maybe his car *is* a dream,
the thin air of the Andes
Don Sergio steers with his feet.
The poet needs no compass, no steering wheel.

His feet already know the way.

the red sea

for Charles Lillard

I would like to mail this thought
through an Easter morning
thick with pollen
swirling in the wind of your leaving,
my friend, to you.

Remember the story I told you.
My son was planting trees on a mountain
and there were blackflies everywhere.
He said it was like
the biblical time of locusts.
My son threw off his boot
and threw it, and where it flew,
the flies parted like the Red Sea.
That was the summer he became a man,
because his boot made a space
large enough for a man to walk through.

You were a man who breathed nature
and the smell of your feet
at the end of the day
when your boots came off
and at last you were able
to walk into the cool water
and refresh yourself.

Whatever made us think a man like you,
with flaming hair, **wouldn't** stand and rage
in a spring storm of petal and seed
like one of those candles
we can't blow out,
no matter how hard we breathe,
wouldn't believe the comet
dragging you across the sky
on the morning of Maundy Thursday,
(it had to be you with your red hair)
was the fire of Pentecost,
wouldn't follow his own boots
into water furious as horses.

You loved the water, shadow weather,
the rocking boats, islands,
the woman shapes that come out of the water
when even you, who refused,
like the angel of light,
to lie down, lay down.

MAGNETIC DIRT

The child attached a magnet to string.
This used to be easy
when string was rolled into balls

in the kitchen drawer,
saved for Armageddon
or some other time down the road,
when the child might wander,
follow candy into the forest,
and need the string to find his way home,
back to his mother,
hanging her laundry out in the sun.

His mother was bright and shiny,
a yellow dress, the sun behind her,
outlining her legs in a family photograph,
the same legs that won her a screen test
in the year before midnight,
when her coachmen turned into mice,
and the mice into dust under her bed.

When his mother unwrapped
meat from the butcher,
she gathered the string,
imagined she was a spider
with eight arms or legs,
all of them frantic, crocheting
things that collected dirt.

She pulled her days through dust—
weeds to be hoed, floors to be swept,
while the child attached his magnet to a string
and dragged it over the garden,
attracting treasure,
magnetic dirt he kept on a shelf
in one of her canning jars.

When his mother went to spirit
he did not bury her in earth
she resisted every day of her life.
Metal attracts metal,
a locket, a tooth filled with gold,
a gold wedding band. He pulled his magnet
through these familiar things
and gathered the light.

the artists of bangladesh

When I close my eyes and see the damaged
girls of Bangladesh,
up to their necks in water,
their shapes distorted
in the monsoon-swollen rivers,
I remember the great painters
who reinvented the women they loved,
their pencils, a line of music,
following the idea of perfection
the way children lie down on pieces of paper
as large as a child and trace one another,
learning the innocent shapes of their bodies.

I see the line as a fugue that always
goes back to the beginning,
where a man with the rain on his side
gets to draw exactly what he wants.
My mother once told me
there were men with cameras
who would steal your soul
in a single exposure and others
who would ask you up to their rooms
so you could see etchings of women,
their lips and eyes exposed to acid,
irrevocably fixed in metal plates.

She showed me etchings by Ingres
and Picasso, who put out cigarettes
in the flesh of his mistress,
and told me the stories of other women
frozen in time by men who made what we see.

She gave me a pencil and told me
women who write poetry
are free to invent themselves
and draw the portraits
of blind, unmarriageable girls,
their faces disfigured by acid,
their only crime being beautiful
and desired by men they refused,
the artists of Bangladesh,
who wash themselves in the flood
waters of the holy Brahmaputra
River and never come clean.

what she said

Her mother taught her to speak
the language of crocodile mothers
and daughters navigating the swamp,
making the squeak of new shoes
rubbing together, saying in unison,
There's no purse like a mother,
crocodile lips carrying her whole
family safely over the water
from her island nest to a mangrove
tree with roots that reach
to the centre of the earth—
her favourite, her only, daughter
riding the matriarch's forehead,
so you'd think she was Queen of the Nile.

She was the jewel in her crocodile
Mama's crocodile crown.

High on her mother's forehead,
she was the third eye, she
was the periscope, she
was the burning bush, the hot
daughter, the one and only
girl speaking in tongues,
the pig-latin crocodile dialect,
holy, holy, her mother's
louder than all the homilies
other girls with patent leather,
not crocodile, shoes
were forced to learn by heart.

The first was *open your big mouth wide,*
as wide as you can,
wider than the squeak of two shoes
rubbing together, because
there were still undiscovered,
unimaginable worlds under her tongue.

She loved the taste of crystal caves.
She loved the sand and salty
flavour of Atlantis and Samarkand,
the jewelled plains of Arabia.

While other crocodile children,
hanging on with their baby teeth,
twisted their infant
bodies in murky tropical waters
and fed on the bodies of mothers,
the water parted for her and her mouth
full of the lonely planet.

None of it tasted like milk.

the last word

Now she is sovereign, first person plural,

in the middle of a war, the ancient game of Go.

The stones are male and female, black and white.

She is no longer afraid of drowning,

naming the game, her turn,

she says *evolution*,

the four winds blowing her backwards,

down past white beds of white flowers,

lily, freesia, narcissus,

pale in her white linen dress,

writing in the shade,

the words moving backwards, into her pen,

past the androgynous gardener,

Jesus, past where her husband

bangs his face on the holy stones

of that ancient wall in Jerusalem,

past the dark shapes on her white nursery wall,

down to the time when she's backing into the swamp—

a reptile with only one bone in her ear.

This is the end game.

Now she's a pen in the hand of God.

The philosopher stones are sewn in her pockets.

She is down to words of one syllable now,

dissolving history, a woman shaped like an inkstone,

becoming transparent,

sipping the river that leads to the ocean,

tasting light as it passes through water.

The last word is love, *agape*, the gulp of freedom

a Chinese concubine swallows

when she's thrown in a well, stones in her pockets,

opium tucked safe under her tongue,

the way a girl is meant to be put to bed,

safe, and it blooms, at last,

a chrysanthemum in her throat.

mother board

All over the world, there is trouble
when girls stand still for light—
Chinese girls, their feet bound in silk,
when they are distracted by sunshine;
African children, cut by their mothers,
unable to run or cry for help;
Inuit women, who doze in the Arctic sun
for a moment, then wake up
and find themselves frozen on igloos.

In French, there is the word *espalier*,
meaning *trained to grow flat on a trellis*.
Men think of Jesus, of course,
and pilgrims to Rome,
their walking sticks sprouting leaves.
Like pilgrims or released domestic pets
who still believe in walls,
girls circle the garden, moving their lips,
remembering the reptile letters e, and s,
then p as the mouth resists,
before opening: aah.

EEEEEEESSSSSSSSSSSSSSPPPPPPPEEEEEEESSSPPPPPPPPPPPPPPPPEEEEEPS
SSSSSSSSSSSSSSSEEEEEEESESESPEPEPEPSSSPEPPEPSPESPEEEEEEPSPSPP,
'PPPPPEEEEESSSSSSSSSEPEPEPEPSPPSSSSSPPPEEEEPPSPPSPPSPPEPEPE

Men wait for this, their ears
alert the way women listen when men
beat their drums in vanishing forests.
When the word begins, they key in the letters;
e, then s and p.
This is the algorithm for God, they think,
the girls perhaps choosing
to ripen on sunny walls
as the mother boards respond,
transmitting the thought, *espalier*,
especially the throat
sound at the end of the world,
where men and women sound like themselves

ESPESPPPPPPPPPEESSSSSESPPEPSPEPSPSPEPEPPPEPPPPPPPEEEEEEEES
PSPSEEPEPEPSSSPPPPPPPEPEPPEPEPSPSPPEPSPSPEPSPPEPSPSPPPPPPEI
SPPEPSESPESPESPESPESPESPESPESPESPESPESPEEEEEESSSSSSSPPPPF

running numbers
in dream time

The swamp is a lottery too.
When dreamtime comes, the water heats up
and all the fish lie on their sides,
one eye on heaven, reading the holy numbers,
clouds rolling by without a care in the world,
and count them, the clouds moving faster
than people in subways, swifter than eagles,
claws ready to carry them off
as soon as one eye closes.

Someone is burning the impenetrable grass.
A small bird, circling her bower,
counts her children,
grieves her shells and her flowers.
She and the fire are the only
music for the Apocalypse.
When the rain comes, the grass
will grow back. Someone has painted
his body white, and drawn,
on the bark of trees,
pictures of animals living in dreamtime.

He has eaten kangaroo meat
　and it helps him dream the dream
　　that everyone in his family is safe.
　　　He counts his ancestors' hands
　　　　stencilled on rocks.
　　　　　He leads his children to the rock
　　　　　　and teaches them to spit the paint.
　　　　　　　The rock is hot and the paint dries quickly.
　　　　　　　Everything with wings is flying.
　　　　　　The fish are gasping for air

Someone has grey hair on his chest.
　His semen is milky, the colour of paint.
　　He goes home and makes love to his wife
　　　waiting in the shade,
　　　　while the children in his family,
　　　　　too young to eat kangaroo meat,
　　　　　　which gives them dreams they can't understand,
　　　　　　　go into the swamp and lie down,
　　　　　　　　one eye on heaven, reading the holy numbers,
　　　　　　　　　clouds rolling by without a care in the world.

It starts with knitting and purling,
a woman dropping a stitch
shaped like a noose
while a man builds a gallows
for someone else and hangs himself.
The book of memorable deeds
dictates the story of Esther
who sang in the bed of her enemy
and revealed the inside of her mouth
pink as a cave full of newborn bats.

Bats and biblical queens
have long sleeves and beautiful fingers.
They hang upside down
playing their harps all night long—
nocturnes for the right hand only—
songs for children
mutilated in the fields of war,
where they have been sent to pick flowers
for the feast of Purim,
when little girls dressed like queens
celebrate in the street cafés of ancient cities.

All this is observed by poets
knitting and purling in space—no time
to intercede for an infant
wearing the same hungry pink as bats
raging in their caves
in the moment before she is separated
from her own right hand
and her mother's lifeless breast
by a human torch
who fell out of the blue Mediterranean sky
onto the daughters of Esther.

Poets orbit the earth, looking for symmetry.
What can they write home about this crooked child
and the waiter attempting to balance
an orphan glass of water on his tray
as he walks among the dead?

the angel of castlegar

On the sixth of August,
I held a second-hand woman in my hand.
She was made of tarnished brass
and men are supposed to remove their boots
in the space between her legs.

The junk store was full of moted light,
the kind that makes you notice
dust from old furniture and books is beautiful
on its way to becoming something else.
The Rinpoche sat on a carved elephant stool and laughed
when my husband made the noise of a baby elephant.
The Lama likes you, someone said. *He will come
to visit you in another lifetime.*

The weather was hot. We had seen thunder clouds.
One, shaped liked a woman, perhaps an angel
I called The Angel of Castlegar,
stood three thousand feet in the sky,
one foot in the Monashee Mountains,
the other in the Kootenay River.
The angel's head was radiant,
surrounded by neon and indigo lines,
a Maltese Cross pointing to our friend's garden.
She might have been wearing a kimono,
her arms flowing into her skirt.

The day was Obon, the Japanese festival
when candles are floated for the dead,
and the anniversary of Hiroshima,
something we are too young to remember,
even though the rain was black.

It was too hot to make love on the ground.
We climbed the mountain, you said, the way
fish throw themselves upriver to spawn,
past bruising rapids and rocks.

We lay down under a tree with cool branches.
The boy from Nakusp who thought he was a wolverine
howled in the forest and a one-eyed
waitress we met in the mountains
made blueberry pie in the dark
while our children crossed the Strait of Georgia
in a boat surrounded by lightning.

We ate lemons, sucking the fruit,
passing the taste back and forth,
saw fish flashing, the fireworks
from Grand Forks the night before,
spirit wrestlers lighting up the sky,
and our children with their children
burying their faces in the soft
spaces at the base of their necks.

The sky was dangerous and we made love
on top of a mountain you said was holy
because the Rinpoche Lama laughed.
You made the sound of a baby elephant for him
and I never loved you more.

In the morning, a woman from Salmon Arm was dead.
Our children were safe on the other side of the gulf,
the tree on the mountain was split down the middle
and the mountain was just a hotel
for people like us, passing through.

lost
and found

Keep one eye on the laying hen
your daughter saved when the neighbour
tried to slit its throat with a knife.
Keep the other on your daughter,
walking into the ocean,
holding her breath,
digging your neighbour's knife
in the lost and found
where deeper mysteries sleep.

Your daughter thinks she sees God
in the golden eye of a carp,
or is it the sun
making you wish you were wearing a hat
where you sit on that log,
getting high on nutmeg tea,
eating scones—one egg from the hen,
a cup of flour, and your own milk,
expressed in a cracked china bowl
with painted fish—
turning to precious stones,
even as your neighbour's knife
gleams in the water,
even as your daughter
finds a petrified seed
that came all the way from Japan,
and searches for the lucky sea-tumbled amethysts
you gave her father when you found him,
cold as a fish with a hook in his mouth,
and which he lost the night
he burned the story of his life on the beach.

She must find the bracelet.
Your lives depend on it.

One egg at a time,
the lady inside the petrified seed
reveals herself.
For two thousand years,
she's been revising the morning after
poem she was writing
when her long-sleeved silk
kimono caught fire
and burned her rice paper
house full of ladybugs to the ground.

Keep your eye on the hen.
She is changing her shape.
Keep your eye on your daughter.
Any minute now, she will burst from the ocean
like a magnolia with jewelled branches,
her father's amethysts in one hand,
the key to an ancient
door in the other.